Discovering
the
Caribbean

BARBADOS

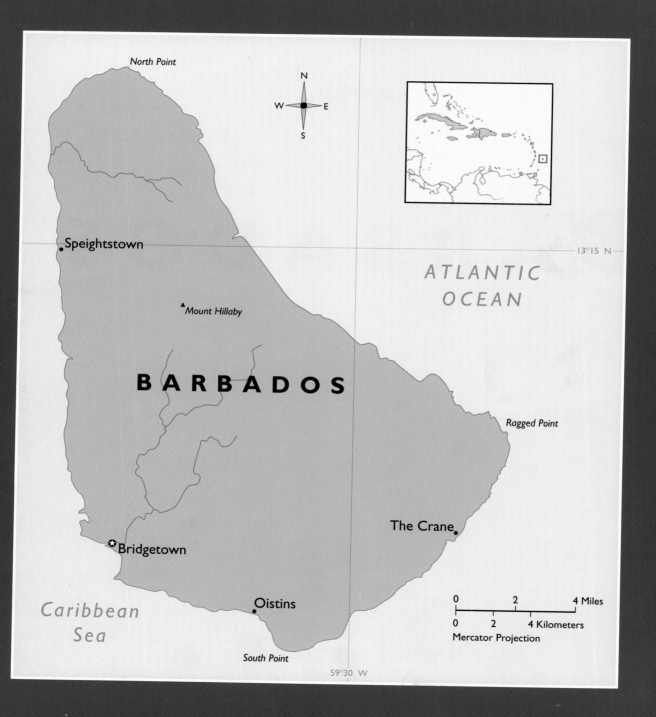

North Point

N
W   E
S

Speightstown

▲ *Mount Hillaby*

BARBADOS

13°15 N

ATLANTIC OCEAN

Ragged Point

The Crane

✪ Bridgetown

Caribbean Sea

Oistins

South Point

59°30 W

0   2   4 Miles
0   2   4 Kilometers
Mercator Projection

Discovering
the
Caribbean

BARBADOS

Tamra Orr

Mason Crest Publishers
Philadelphia

Produced by OTTN Publishing, Stockton, N.J.

Mason Crest Publishers
370 Reed Road
Broomall, PA 19008
www.masoncrest.com

First printing

1 3 5 7 9 8 6 4 2

Library of Congress Cataloging-in-Publication Data

   Orr, Tamra.
    Barbados / Tamra Orr.
      p. cm. — (Discovering the Caribbean)
   Summary: Presents information on the geography, history, economy, and people of
   Barbados. Includes a chronology, recipes, project ideas, and more.
   Includes bibliographical references and index.
    ISBN 1-59084-306-1
   1. Barbados—Juvenile literature. [1. Barbados.] I. Title. II. Series.
   F2041 .O76 2003b
   972.981—dc21

                                                2002011893

Discovering the Caribbean

Bahamas
Barbados
Cuba
Dominican Republic
Haiti

Caribbean Islands:
Facts & Figures

Jamaica
Leeward Islands
Puerto Rico
Trinidad & Tobago
Windward Islands

Table of Contents

Discovering the Caribbean

James D. Henderson

THE CARIBBEAN REGION is a lovely, ethnically diverse part of tropical America. It is at once a sea, rivaling the Mediterranean in size; and it is islands, dozens of them, stretching along the sea's northern and eastern edges. Waters of the Caribbean Sea bathe the eastern shores of Central America's seven nations, as well as those of the South American countries Colombia, Venezuela, and Guyana. The Caribbean islands rise, like a string of pearls, from its warm azure waters. Their sandy beaches, swaying palm trees, and balmy weather give them the aspect of tropical paradises, intoxicating places where time seems to stop.

But it is the people of the Caribbean region who make it a unique place. In their ethnic diversity they reflect their homeland's character as a crossroads of the world for more than five centuries. Africa's imprint is most visible in peoples of the Caribbean, but so too is that of Europe. South and East Asian strains enrich the Caribbean ethnic mosaic as well. Some islanders reveal traces of the region's first inhabitants, the Carib and Taino Indians, who flourished there when Columbus appeared among them in 1492.

Though its sparkling waters and inviting beaches beckon tourists from around the globe, the Caribbean islands provide a significant portion of the world's sugar, bananas, coffee, cacao, and natural fibers. They are strategically important also, for they guard the Panama Canal's eastern approaches.

The Caribbean possesses a cultural diversity rivaling the ethnic kaleido-scope that is its human population. Though its dominant culture is Latin American, defined by languages and customs bequeathed it by Spain and France, significant parts of the Caribbean bear the cultural imprint of

A view of the ocean through a palm grove, Barbados.

Northwestern Europe: Denmark, the Netherlands, and most significantly, Britain.

So welcome to the Caribbean! These lavishly illustrated books survey the human and physical geography of the Caribbean, along with its economic and historical development. Geared to the needs of students and teachers, each of the eleven volumes in the series contains a glossary of terms, a chronology, and ideas for class reports. And each volume contains a recipe section featuring tasty, easy-to-prepare dishes popular in the countries dealt with. Each volume is indexed, and contains a bibliography featuring web sources for further information.

Whether old or young, readers of the eleven-volume series DISCOVERING THE CARIBBEAN will come away with a new appreciation of this tropical sea, its jewel-like islands, and its fascinating and friendly people!

(Opposite) Gun Hill signal station in St. George Parish is one of six outposts built by the British during the early 19th century. (Right) The Atlantic Ocean washes the beach at Bathsheba, on the scenic eastern coast of Barbados.

1 Beauty, Beaches, and Bajans

DOTTING THE EASTERN Caribbean are a chain of islands, each with its own unique history, flavor, and communities. On the easterly side of this chain—the Lesser Antilles—is Barbados, an island of beauty, beaches, and fascinating people called Bajans (or Barbadians).

Barbados is not a large island. It is approximately 21 miles (34 kilometers) long and 14 miles (23 km) wide—or about the size of a large city in the United States. The island is roughly triangular in shape (some people say it looks like a lopsided pear or a pear-shaped emerald). To the southwest is the Caribbean Sea; to the northeast, the Atlantic Ocean. Barbados is located about 1,600 miles (2,575 km) southeast of Miami, Florida; 535 miles (861 km) northeast of Caracas, Venezuela; and 4,200 miles (6,759 km) from its biggest influence—London, England. And unlike the other Caribbean islands, Barbados was not found or named by Christopher Columbus!

Despite its small size, Barbados is home to many people. In fact, it is one of the most crowded countries in the world. Why do people want to live on this triangle-shaped island? A few reasons, among many, may be the lush vegetation, the coral reefs, the sandy beaches, and the warm tropical breezes.

A Look Around

Most of Barbados is flat, although there is a gentle rise in the center of the island. Unlike the other islands of the Caribbean, which are primarily volcanic, Barbados is a low-lying island atop a coral limestone formation that geologists think may be close to 600,000 years old. The entire island is surrounded by coral reefs. These help protect the island from the continuing push of the ocean's waves. However, in recent years pollution has been breaking down these reefs

Delicate orchids at the Andromeda Botanic Garden. Many kinds of orchids grow on Barbados.

and damaging the beaches. In the mid-1980s, the government of Barbados set up a conservation program to help stop this process.

While other islands in the Lesser Antilles tend to have mountains, Barbados does not. Its highest point, Mount Hillaby, rises only 1,104 feet (337 meters). From this height climbers can look down on much of the island. Steep hills can be seen stretching in several directions, becoming smaller and gentler as they slope toward the sea.

The white, sandy beaches of Barbados lure thousands of tourists to the island each year. The southern coast's Casuarina Beach features the biggest waves and is the favorite spot for windsurfers, while Sandy Beach on the northern coast has quieter waters and attracts families. Payne's Bay is the place to go to on the western coast if you enjoy snorkeling and other water sports, and the best swimming can be found at Church Point on the western coast.

How's the Weather?

People from all over the world like to vacation on Barbados, and one of the main reasons is the weather. With more than 3,000 hours of sunshine each year, it is almost always warm and sunny. No matter the month, the high temperature is usually around 85°F (29°C), while lows rarely dip below 70°F (21°C). The rainy season is between June and November. Three-quarters of the annual rainfall—about 60 inches (152 centimeters), on average—occurs during these months.

Hurricanes are the only real natural hazard on Barbados. While most of these seasonal storms tend to bypass Barbados and head off to the north, some do hit the island. When they do, incredible damage can result. Strong

Quick Facts: The Geography of Barbados

Location: island between the Caribbean Sea and the North Atlantic Ocean, northeast of Venezuela

Area: (about 2.5 times the size of Washington, D.C.)
  total: 166 square miles (266 sq km)
  land: 166 square miles (266 sq km)
  water: 0 square miles

Borders: none

Climate: tropical; rainy season June through October

Terrain: relatively flat with a gentle rise to the central highland region

Elevation extremes:
  lowest point: Atlantic Ocean—0 feet
  highest point: Mt. Hillaby—1,104 feet (337 meters)

Natural hazards: hurricanes, landslides

Source: Adapted from CIA World Factbook 2001.

hurricanes pounded Barbados in 1780, 1831, 1898, and, most recently, 1955. Each time they killed many people and destroyed crops, businesses, and homes. Hurricanes and tropical storms come during the summer months.

Plants and Trees of Barbados

While other islands in this part of the world are home to many unusual types of plants and flowers, Barbados is not. Much of the island's native plant life is extinct, thanks to the massive crop planting and cultivation done by early settlers. Over a quarter of the island's land is devoted to sugarcane fields.

Large fig trees, which are native to the island, can still be found along its shores. These trees have a thick, cascading canopy of vines that resemble a man's beard and inspired the island's name. The 16th-century Portuguese explorer Pedro a Campos called the island "Los Barbados," meaning "the bearded ones." Other trees that are native to Barbados include the Bajan ebony, clammy cherry, calabash, West Indian almond, willow lavender, pop-a-gun, and sandbox trees.

Fruit trees, such as mango, coconut, guava, and cherry trees, grow on Barbados. Unusual kinds of apples, such as the star apple, the golden apple, and the sugar apple, can also be found on the island. Mangrove forests grow along the coasts, providing homes to sponges, corals, oysters, fish, lobsters, and many kinds of nesting birds. Flowers thrive on Barbados, and many different kinds of orchids grow on the island; many are on display at Orchid World in St. George Valley. The national flower is the Pride of Barbados, or *Caesal pinia pulchermia*, a red flower with yellow borders.

Over the years Europeans brought other unusual trees to the island. These include the mahogany, the tamarind, the casuarinas, the cabbage palm, and the African tulip. The baobab, or "monkey-bread" tree, is believed

The Crane Beach Hotel, built in 1887, was the first resort on Barbados. It can be found at one of the island's most attractive spots.

Many types of fish can be found in the waters around Barbados, such as this flying fish just caught in St. Peter, on the northern coast.

to have been brought to Barbados from Africa around 1738. This tree has a trunk that can grow to 45 feet around. No one is sure exactly how the tree got to Barbados. It is possible that seeds were carried on ships with African slaves.

One of the best places to see all the plants and flowers that Barbados has to offer is the Flower Forest, 12 miles northeast of Bridgetown. Here you will find more than 50 acres of flora, along with incredible views of the Chalky Mountains and the Atlantic Ocean. The Andromeda Botanic Gardens on the east coast also showcases the island's plants and flowers for visitors.

The Fauna

Barbados has very few native animal species. However, the island is home to a grass snake that is not found anywhere else in the world, as well as a blind snake. Other unusual animals are blackbelly sheep, red-footed tortoises, and eight different kinds of bats. On the island butterflies are called bats, while bats are referred to as leather bats. Two dozen species of birds reside on the island, including the Caribbean grackle and the bananaquit. Another 180 types of birds migrate to Barbados for part of the year. Six kinds of reptiles and amphibians live on Barbados, including a one-inch-long whistling frog that makes a high-pitched humming noise. The sea surrounding Barbados is home to 17 different kinds of sea urchins, plus starfish, sponges, jellyfish, and many types of tropical fish.

European settlers brought some animals to the island. Perhaps the most visible of these is the green monkey, which arrived on Barbados about 350 years ago. Averaging 16 to 18 inches in length, plus tail, these black-faced creatures are considered pests. In fact, at one time the government paid residents a reward for each monkey tail they brought in. Today, there are about 10,000 green monkeys on Barbados. Another imported animal is the mongoose, originally brought to the island to help get rid of rats.

The Barbados Wildlife Reserve, located 16 miles (26 km) north of Bridgetown, is a great place to see many of the island's animals. A pathway takes tourists through the woods, where they can observe monkeys, tortoises, and other creatures. An *aviary* in the reserve features everything from macaws and cockatoos to peacocks and pelicans.

(Opposite) Palms surround a colonial-style residence at Cobbler's Grove. (Right) This replica of a pirate ship is docked at Holetown.

2 Little England of the Caribbean

BARBADOS TODAY IS an intriguing mixture of African and British cultures. A quick look at the history of this Caribbean island makes it easy to understand why.

The first inhabitants of Barbados were Amerindians, as natives of the Western Hemisphere before the arrival of Europeans are called. In the late 1990s, archaeologists discovered the remains of an ancient culture of fishermen who lived on Barbados and used tools made from *conch shells*. Using the technique of *radiocarbon dating*, scientists were able to establish that these people lived on the island as early as 5,000 years ago.

Several thousand years later, between 400 and 200 B.C., the Arawaks— Amerindians who came from South America—arrived on the island. They were farmers, fishermen, and pottery makers. The Arawaks occupied

In 1625 English explorers landed on Barbados and claimed the island for their king, James I.

Barbados until sometime around A.D. 1200, when they mysteriously disappeared. One theory is that they were wiped out by the Caribs, a fierce, warlike tribe that spread from present-day Venezuela throughout northern South America and the Caribbean.

Archaeologists know that the Caribs occupied Barbados for about 300 years before they, too, disappeared. Though no records exist to confirm it, some were probably captured by Spanish or Portuguese soldiers and taken from the island to work as slaves in mines or on plantations. Smallpox and other diseases Europeans brought with them to the New World may have killed the rest. Because these diseases did not exist in the Western Hemisphere before the arrival of the Europeans, Amerindians had no immunity to them. Thus exposure had devastating consequences for the native population.

The British Arrive

When the British arrived on Barbados in 1625, they found nobody living on the island. Captain John Powell claimed the land for England in the name of King James I. Two years later, Powell's brother Henry led an expedition to the island. In February 1627, Henry Powell's ship *William and Mary* landed on Barbados's west coast, at the present-day location of Holetown. The 80 Englishmen and 10 slaves aboard disembarked and set about establishing a settlement, which grew quickly as more people arrived from England. Within a year, the population of the island had grown to 2,000.

The new settlers thought of Barbados as their own little England—albeit a tropical England. Wealthy Britons who were suffering from health problems or depression sailed to the island for warmth and relaxation. Other immigrants came to escape England's civil wars (1639–40 and 1642–51). In 1639, a parliament was established on Barbados to act as the island's governing body, and Barbados was divided into 11 *parishes*, or administrative divisions.

The first colonists had focused on clearing the land and planting tobacco and cotton, but the 1640s saw a shift from those crops to sugarcane. Sugarcane grew very well on the island, and soon the plantation owners wanted to expand in order to make more money. But they would need more workers to clear the forests and tend the larger sugarcane fields they envisioned.

The English residents of Barbados solved their labor problems by importing black slaves from Africa. Between 1640 and 1807, almost 400,000 African slaves were brought to Barbados. By the 1650s, slaves outnumbered their white masters by two to one. Within 30 more years, that ratio had increased to four blacks for every white person on the island. The African influence would soon be felt in everything from the island's music to its food and clothing.

Did You Know?

- George Washington visited Barbados in 1751 with his brother Lawrence, who was seeking a cure for his tuberculosis. It was the only time the future general and first president of the United States ever traveled outside America.

- During its colonial period, Barbados's coat of arms contained a trident, a three-pronged spear that in classical mythology was wielded by the god of the sea (Poseidon in the Greek pantheon; Neptune in the Roman pantheon). The current flag of Barbados—two vertical bands of blue bracketing a gold band—contains just the head of a trident. This symbolizes the country's break with its past and its independence.

- Barbados is a sovereign country within the British Commonwealth. As such, its official head of state is the English monarch, Queen Elizabeth II, who appoints a governor-general to represent the crown's interests on the island. In turn, the governor-general appoints the Barbadian prime minister, who is the country's head of government.

- In total area, Barbados is only two and a half times larger than the city of Washington, D.C. It has fewer than half as many residents as the District of Columbia.

Years of Growth and Change

By the middle of the 17th century, the plantations and their owners were prospering. The island's population continued to grow as more people came to settle there. Cities were formed and expanded quickly.

Life was far from perfect, however. Sugar ants ruined crops in 1760. Six years later, a huge fire destroyed most of the capital, Bridgetown. A hurricane in 1780 also damaged many buildings and homes. Still later, a smallpox epidemic killed many people. Despite these problems, the island community grew.

The 19th century brought changes to Barbados. The government of England declared the slave trade illegal in 1807. However, this did not give the slaves already living on Barbados their freedom. It took until 1834 for the *emancipation* of slaves on the island to become a reality. Unfortunately, freedom did little to improve the poor living conditions of the blacks on Barbados. Though no longer slaves, blacks did not enjoy the same rights as white residents of the island. Because there were few jobs other than plantation work, many blacks continued toiling in the fields for low wages.

In 1876, black Bajans held a large protest because they did not have the right to vote for the island's rulers. Several of the protest's organizers were killed, and more than 400 participants were thrown in jail.

Barbados faced health and weather-related challenges as well during the 19th and early 20th centuries. Major hurricanes struck the island in 1831 and 1898, killing thousands. An epidemic of *cholera* swept Barbados in 1854, claiming more than 20,000 lives. In 1902, smallpox again devastated the population, and six years later a deadly epidemic of yellow fever broke out.

A New Century

As the 20th century began, Barbados was still a colony of Great Britain. Sugar remained the most important part of the island's economy. This was fine when the price of sugar was stable. However, World War I and other international problems caused sugar prices to fluctuate. By the 1930s, the Great

Depression was affecting many countries throughout the world. A 50 percent drop in sugar prices wreaked havoc on Barbados, resulting in widespread unemployment and hard times for many Bajans, especially blacks.

After riots erupted in the streets of Barbados, the government of Great Britain established the Colonial Welfare and Development Office. This agency provided money to Barbados and other British colonies in the Caribbean. The British also gave black residents of the island a greater say in the political process. A man named Grantley Adams, who had helped direct social protests, formed the Barbados Labour Party in 1938.

After World War II ended in 1945, many changes took place in Great Britain's colonies, including Barbados. Adams became the island's first premier in 1954, and he worked hard to change both the culture and the constitution. In 1961, Great Britain gave the island's government complete control over internal affairs. Five years later, in 1966, Barbados was finally granted independence from Great Britain, with Errol Barrow serving as the new nation's prime minister.

Although no longer a colony, Barbados maintained ties to Great Britain. It became a member country in the British Commonwealth of Nations. It was also accepted as a member of the United Nations. In 1967, Barbados joined the Organization of America States.

Barrow remained the prime minister for a decade, until 1976. During that time, he worked to improve education, labor relations, health care, and social security on Barbados. He also promoted tourism. In 1985, Barrow led his Democratic Labour Party back to power and again served as prime minister until his death in office in 1987.

Grantley Adams (1898–1971) was an important leader in the movement for Barbados's independence from Great Britain. He served as the first premier of Barbados (1954–58), and as prime minister of the West Indies Federation (1958–62).

In 1994, Owen Arthur became prime minister. Trained as an economist, Arthur promoted economic integration among the Caribbean nations. He was reappointed in 1999 for a second term.

Legislature and Judiciary

The legislative branch of Barbados consists of a two-chamber Parliament. The 21 members of the Senate are appointed by the governor-

Cuban president Fidel Castro (right) presents Owen Arthur, the prime minister of Barbados, with the José Martí Award, Cuba's highest honor, on June 16, 1999, in Havana. Barbados has attempted to keep good relations with its Caribbean neighbors; the island is a member of the Organization of American States, the Association of Caribbean States, and the Caribbean Community (Caricom).

general. The 28 members of the House of Assembly are elected to five-year terms by popular vote.

At the head of the country's judicial branch is the Supreme Court of Judicature. Its judges are appointed by Barbados's Service Commissions for the Judicial and Legal Services.

Wide Appeal

Today Barbados is a place that attracts businesses and politicians from all over the world. U.S. president Ronald Reagan and his wife Nancy visited in 1982, and President Bill Clinton visited in 1997. Visitors from every corner of the world vacation there also. All seem to appreciate the unique blend of English and African cultures that is part of Barbados's heritage.

(Opposite) A farmer gathers the harvest. The major crops on Barbados are sugarcane and cotton. (Right) Rum has been a mainstay of the island's economy for hundreds of years. Today, visitors can tour a modern distillery at Heritage Park.

3 From Sugar to Tourists

THE ECONOMY OF Barbados has gone through many changes in its long history. Although the island was once a major producer of sugar, today tourism makes up the biggest part of the economy. Barbados has beauty and beaches— and Bajans welcome foreigners who want to experience the natural treasures of their island. In addition, during the past 20 years, many international corporations have built new facilities and factories in Barbados, making it a center for banking, pharmaceutical, and information technology companies.

Not surprisingly, Barbados—a country of only about 275,000 citizens—has a rather small economy. Using a method designed to account for local variations in the cost of living (called purchasing power parity), its *gross domestic product (GDP)* for the year 2001 was estimated at just

$4 billion. (GDP is the total value of goods and services produced in a country in a one-year period.) By comparison, the GDP of the Dominican Republic, another Caribbean nation, stood at an estimated $50 billion; GDP in the United States, the world's largest economy, topped $10 *trillion*.

But GDP is largely a function of a nation's population. Despite the small overall size of Barbados's economy, the typical Bajan is comparatively well off. Per capita GDP—each citizen's average share of the nation's economic activity—was estimated at $14,500 in 2001. Estimates for some other Caribbean nations in the same year were: Haiti, $1,700; Cuba, $2,300; Jamaica, $3,700; the Dominican Republic, $5,800. Per capita GDP in the United Kingdom, from which Barbados has inherited so much culturally, was estimated at $24,700, while in the United States the figure was $36,000.

The Importance of Sugar

In the early years of its colonial era, the main source of money for Barbados was its sugarcane industry. Introduced in the 1640s, this crop quickly surpassed the cotton and tobacco crops in both yield and profit. It also changed the entire makeup of the island. Instead of just a few English settlers working small farms, there was a huge increase in population as thousands of slaves were brought over from Africa to work the large sugarcane plantations.

For the next 300 years, sugar and its *by-products*—rum and molasses—kept the economy of Barbados alive. Over a quarter of the entire island was covered with sugarcane plantations. Many Englishmen found themselves rich because of this one crop. Unfortunately, if the price of sugar went down,

A Bajan waiter serves drinks to tourists lying on the beach. Tourism has become one of the most important parts of Barbados's economy. More than a million people visit Barbados each year, and 20 percent of the island's population is employed in tourism-related jobs.

the island's entire economy declined also. Sugar prices tended to rise and fall constantly, making for unstable times for everyone in Barbados. Occasional hurricanes took a toll on the economy as well, destroying homes and businesses. The island's history of smallpox, cholera, and yellow fever epidemics also affected the output of the sugar plantations.

The price of sugar dropped dramatically during the 1930s, but rebounded slightly during the Second World War. After the war, sugar prices fell again. This time, the decline was slow but steady. By the late 1980s, many of the sugar plantations had fallen into bankruptcy.

A vendor sells coconuts near King's Beach Hotel in St. Peter.

Quick Facts: The Economy of Barbados

Gross domestic product (GDP*):
$4 billion (purchasing power parity)
GDP per capita: $14,500 (purchasing power parity)
Inflation: 3.5%
Natural resources: petroleum, fish, natural gas
Agriculture (6% of GDP): sugarcane, cotton (2000 est.)
Services (78% of GDP): tourism, banking and insurance, information services (2000 est.)
Industry (16% of GDP): pharmaceuticals, light manufacturing (2000 est.)

*GDP = the total value of goods and services produced in one year.

Foreign trade (2000):
Exports: $272 million—sugar, molasses, rum, foods, beverages, chemicals, electronic components, clothing.
Imports: $1.16 billion—consumer goods, machinery, foodstuffs, construction materials, fuel, electronic components.
Currency exchange rate: 1 Barbados dollar (BBD) = U.S. $0.50 (fixed rate pegged to the U.S. dollar)

Figures are 2001 estimates unless otherwise indicated. Source: Adapted from the CIA World Factbook 2002.

The sugar industry continues to play an economic role in Barbados, but it is a fairly minor one. The St. George Valley in central Barbados has working sugar estates, often controlled by the same families that started them hundreds of years ago. The plantations produce about a quarter of what they once did, and most of this sugar is sold to Europe.

Cotton fields can still be seen in areas of St. Thomas. The crop, which continues to be picked by hand, is a common export to Japan and the United States.

The Tourism Boom

An increase in tourism to the island filled the void caused by the decline of the sugar industry. People had been visiting the island to relax or improve their health since the 17th century. However, as air travel became more common in the 1960s, the number of tourists visiting Barbados grew quickly. Currently, more than a million people visit this island each year.

Tourism is the core of Barbados's economy. The wonderful, warm weather, sandy beaches, and sunshine beckon people to visit—especially those who enjoy water sports like snorkeling, windsurfing, *parasailing*, fishing, and scuba diving.

Tourism now brings in more than 10 times as much money as the sugar industry. It provides many jobs—today one in five Bajans works in the tourism industry. It has also led the Bajans to expand their harbors and airports to accommodate visitors. About half of the tourists arrive on cruise ships; others come on airplanes such as the Concorde, which touches down from London once a week. It is little surprise that the island's shorelines are now covered with condominiums, shopping centers, hotels, and restaurants.

An Industrial Center

Tourism isn't the only important sector of Barbados's economy. Today, the island's economy is based on a combination of tourism, more than 150 factories, and information technology.

Small-scale manufacturing plants make chemicals, clothing, and electronic products. Processing plants continue to make refined sugar products—rum and molasses—as well as oils, lard, and margarine.

Offshore banking and insurance have become important contributors to the economy, as have online companies and information technology. There are more than 800 international businesses located in Barbados as well as 700 foreign sales corporations and 200 insurance companies. All of them work to receive, process, and report information and transmit it back to the United States. Information technology (software development, medical records processing, telemarketing, direct mail, and so on) has grown so much in the last 15 years that today the island is considered one of the best offshore locations in the world for this kind of industry.

What attracts all these businesses are various incentives, which the government of Barbados has set up specifically to lure companies to the island. These include numerous tax breaks on profits and exports and imports, reasonably priced office and factory rental spaces, educated and easily trained workers, and no requirements to file local tax returns or financial statements.

(Opposite) Students attend a primary school in St. John Parish. Barbados has a literacy rate that is among the highest in Latin America. (Right) Street musicians warm up before a performance at the market in Bridgetown.

4 All o' We Are Bajans!

THE PEOPLE OF Barbados may officially be called Barbadians, but if you ask them, they'll tell you they are Bajans. And there are a lot of them too! With over 275,000 people, the small island is rather crowded. In fact, with about 1,619 people per square mile (625 per sq km), Barbados is among the world's most densely populated nations. Yet, in its 2001 Human Development Report, the United Nations ranked Barbados 30th on its list of the 174 best countries to live in. It led all of the countries in the Americas.

Meet the Bajans

The people of Barbados are almost always friendly. They like to laugh, they enjoy a good joke, and they are usually in no hurry. It's difficult to upset Bajans, who have a well-deserved reputation for being very down-to-earth people.

Eight in 10 Bajans are black; 4 percent are white. The remaining 16 percent of the population is composed of *mulattos* (people of mixed black and white heritage) and a combination of North and South Americans, Syrians, Lebanese, East Indians, and Chinese. Despite the large majority of blacks in Barbados, discrimination persisted until relatively recently. For example, it took until 1970 for the last school on the island to admit blacks as students, and for sports clubs to allow black members.

Life in the typical Bajan home is different from life in most U.S. homes. Many couples live together without marrying, and more than three-quarters of the babies in Barbados are born out of wedlock. Some couples never marry, while others live together for a long time first. A third of those who do marry eventually divorce. It isn't unusual for men and women to go through several live-in relationships before they settle down with one person.

Many households include more than one generation: often grandparents, uncles, and aunts all live together. The grandmother plays a large role within the family, often taking care of her children's children while the adults are busy with other things.

On Barbados, traditional gender roles persist: men go to work, and women, for the most part, stay home and take care of the children. Eighty-five percent of the jobs in Barbados belong to men, although women are slowly trying to change this. More Bajan women are becoming lawyers and businesswomen every year.

Education and Religion

Public education is free in Barbados, and children are required to go to school between the ages of 5 and 16. As a result, the island boasts a remarkably high literacy rate—more than 97 percent of Bajans age 15 and older can read and write. The island has a number of colleges, including the University of the West Indies, Barbados Community College, Codrington College, and the Barbados Institute of Management and Productivity. A sign that times are changing is that more women then men are enrolled at several of the universities.

Religion is a very important part of life for almost all of the people of Barbados. In fact, the island has more churches per square mile than anywhere else in the world. Believers range from Jews, Hindus, and Muslims to Mormons, Catholics, and *Rastafarians*. Somehow, they all manage to get along well together.

Many of the beliefs and superstitions on Barbados have African roots. A belief in

A man walks past a colorful mural at Barbados Community College, one of several institutions of higher education on the island.

duppies, or ghosts, is not unusual, and some islanders will scatter sand around their homes or walk in the door backwards to make sure a duppie doesn't enter. Another belief that some Bajans share is in *obeah*, a form of magic that often involves potions. Some men claim they were married only because their girl-friends gave them an "obeah come to me sauce" when they weren't looking. Others blame obeah when they do something wrong or make a mistake; people have even used it as an excuse when they are on trial for breaking the law.

Music and Art

It is often said that Bajans can dance long before they are able to walk. Music is heard almost everywhere on Barbados—on the radio, in church, on buses, and at home. It is usually a combination of *reggae* from Jamaica and West Indian *calypso*. Many of the songs talk about what is wrong with society, from potholes to politicians. Steel drums give the music an exciting rhythm and beat. This music wasn't always allowed, however. In 1688, the British had drums and other local instruments banned. Instead, the music was played in secret until the 1960s when a group called the Merrymen brought it back. In 1963, Radio Barbados was started, spreading the sound of the music even further. *Tuk* bands became popular; their name came from the *boom-a-tuk* sound their log drums made. Performers like Mighty Gabby and Red Plastic Bag made the music more popular, and today's artists include Romeo, David Kirton, and Viper.

Art is also important to Bajans, and the number of art galleries on the island is increasing. Making beautiful clay pottery has become a Barbados tradition, and many pots are sold to tourists who want something special to

Quick Facts: The People of Barbados

Population: 275,330
Ethnic groups: black, 80%; white, 4%; other (including mulattos, North or South American, Syrian, Lebanese, East Indian, and Chinese), 16%
Age structure:
  0—14 years: 21.68%
  15—64 years: 69.44%
  65 years and over: 8.88%
Population growth rate: 0.46%
Birth rate: 13.47 babies born/1,000 population
Death rate: 8.53/1,000 population
Infant mortality rate: 12.04/1,000 live births

Life expectancy at birth:
  total population: 73.25 years
  male: 70.66 years
  female: 75.86 years
Total fertility rate: 1.64 children born per woman
Religions: Protestant, 67%; Roman Catholic, 4%; none, 17%; other, 12%
Languages: English (official)
Literacy rate (age 15 and older who have attended school): 97.4% (1995 est.)

All figures are 2001 estimates unless otherwise indicated.
Source: Adapted from CIA World Factbook 2001.

take back home. Colorful murals can be seen on the sides of buildings and stores, and sculptures are showing up as well.

The National Passion

Without a doubt, however, the biggest passion for almost all Bajans is the game of cricket. Some even call the game a national religion. Introduced more than 200 years ago by the British military, cricket is an outdoor game played with bats, a ball, and wickets by two teams of 11 players each. In Barbados, cricket is a way of life, from the professional games held in the Oval, which seats 15,000 fans, to casual games played on the island's beaches.

When teams were first put together in Barbados, they were all white. Then, in the 1950s, the Empire Club was formed for blacks and whites. It produced three of the island's best cricket players of all time, the Terrible Three W's: Frank Worrell, Clyde Walcott, and Everton Weekes. They played so well and made such an impression that the queen of England knighted all three of them. Worrell's face can still be found today on the Bajan five-dollar bill.

To this day, Barbados's most famous cricket player is Garfield Sobers, who played from 1958 to 1974 and is considered by some to be the best all-round player in the history of the game. A song written about him in 1965 called him "the greatest cricketer on Earth or on Mars." A national hero, Sobers was knighted in 1975.

Less popular than cricket but still worth noting is road tennis, a game the Bajans invented. It's a lot like Ping-Pong, or table tennis, but with an unusual

Two of Barbados's greatest cricket players: Frank Worrell (left) and Everton Weekes, before a record-breaking match in 1950.

twist. Instead of using the typical Ping-Pong table, Bajans play road tennis anywhere they can find an open piece of concrete. A green playing board is drawn on the ground with white boundary lines, and an eight-inch board is put up as a net. Created in the 1940s as something fun and inexpensive to do, the game has grown so much that tourists can often watch matches going on in open parking lots or quiet side streets. In 1976, the Barbados Road Tennis Association was formed, and now there are tournaments between villages.

A craftsman makes pottery on Barbados.

Dancing in the Streets

Bajans like to celebrate. They hold many festivals throughout the year for tourists and for themselves. Three of the biggest events are the Crop Over, the Da Congaline Carnival, and the Independence Day Festival.

Crop Over usually begins in June and runs through the first week of August. Once held to celebrate the end of the sugarcane harvest, today it is an important part of Bajan culture. Music roars out, parades march by, and fireworks light up the sky.

Da Congaline Carnival, held in late April, has been called "the World's Greatest Street Party." Thousands of dancers in matching outfits snake through the streets in a festive parade.

On Independence Day in late November, artists of all kinds compete for medals and other awards.

(Opposite) An aerial view of Bridgetown, the capital of Barbados. (Right) A Bajan woman wears an ornate costume during the Crop Over Festival, an extended island-wide festival held throughout July that celebrates the completion of the sugarcane harvest.

5 Exploring the Lopsided Pear

BARBADOS IS DIVIDED into 11 separate parishes. Each one has its own towns and cities, flavor, and style, and they are surprisingly individual.

St. Michael

Located in the southwest corner of Barbados, this parish claims about 7,500 residents. The national capital, Bridgetown, is located here. Founded in 1628, Bridgetown is a city with a great history. Today it is the site of most of the island's industry.

Though it has fewer than 7,000 residents, Bridgetown is a busy city filled with contrasts. Rastafarians with their *dreadlocks* can be seen selling their wares to businessmen in suits and ties. Throughout the city old mixes with new. Anglican cathedrals dating from the 17th century stand next to contemporary office buildings. Heroes Square (formerly called Trafalgar Square) is a favorite spot for tourists, and vendors line the nearby streets selling their unique products. On Baxter's Road, nicknamed "the street that never sleeps," visitors can find everything from souvenirs to rum drinks and delicious Barbadian treats.

St. Michael Parish is also home to a 19th-century *synagogue*, the Barbados Museum, the Fountain Gardens, and the Bridgetown Harbor, where up to 2,000 tons of cargo is loaded and unloaded every day. The Barbados Garrison—a 17th-century British naval base, complete with cannons and a *brig*—is also located in the parish.

St. James

The parish of St. James lies on the west coast of the island—an area sometimes called the Gold Coast because it is where the richest tourists and visitors stay. Land sells for more than $3 million per acre here! Even a one-bedroom apartment can cost as much as $500,000. Luxury hotels and gated communities fill the coastline.

St. James Parish includes Holetown, the site of the first English settlement on Barbados. Originally called Jamestown, Holetown hosts a popular festival in February.

Other attractions in St. James Parish include Folkestone Park and Marine Reserve, a marine museum, underwater park, and saltwater aquarium. This parish is home to both the University of the West Indies and the St. James Church, a structure that dates back more than 250 years.

Christic Church

Four miles (6 km) long, this parish on the southern coast includes the communities of Hastings, Worthing, and Dover. The most developed area on

Tourists walk down the road in Bathsheba, a small fishing village in
St. Joseph Parish on Barbados's east coast.

A small settlement nestles atop coastal cliffs in St. Andrew Parish.

the entire island, Christ Church Parish is a favorite of tourists, who are drawn by the many hotels, shopping malls, and restaurants—and by prices that are much more affordable than those found in the Gold Coast area of western Barbados.

Christ Church Parish is home to Oistins, the fishing capital of Barbados. Here you can buy almost any kind of fish, including dolphin, barracuda, snapper, and the island favorite, flying fish. The Graeme Hall Bird Sanctuary is another popular tourist attraction.

St. Philip, St. John, St. Joseph, and St. Andrew

The largest and fastest-growing parish in Barbados is St. Philip, on the southeast coast. Here the coastal beaches are much wilder, with churning water, large waves, and sharp rocks. While not as attractive to tourists as other areas of Barbados, this parish is the location of one of the island's biggest oil fields. Discovered in 1966, this single well produces enough oil to provide more than a third of the island's entire energy needs.

In the eastern portion of the island are three small parishes that tend to blend together—St. John, St. Joseph, and St. Andrew. Tourists don't flock to these parishes, whose beaches are usually empty and whose seas are quite rough.

Codrington College is in St. John Parish, as is the Chalky Mountain Village, home to a generation of potters who live there to be close to the island's largest reserve of clay. Hackleton's Cliff is another highlight of St. John Parish. Rising almost 1,000 feet (305 meters), it offers incredible views in all directions.

St. Thomas

In the heart of the island is the parish of St. Thomas. This area is often called the Scotland District because its rolling hills, incredible views, and rock formations reminded early Scottish settlers of their homeland. Steep, crooked roads limit the traffic in this area; however, tourist attractions still draw visitors. This parish is home to the Flower Forest, Mount Hillaby (the island's highest point), and Rock Hall Village, the first free black village in the country.

Another fascinating spot in this parish is Harrison's Cave, an amazing complex complete with *stalactites*, *stalagmites*, underground waterfalls, and green pools of water. Visitors can see the caves on electric wagons with tour guides.

St. George

Located in the middle of the island, this parish is made up mainly of sugarcane fields that are still being farmed—in many cases by the ancestors of the original owners. The 878-acre Drax Hill Estate was the first sugar plantation established in Barbados. Orchid World is also located in St. George. In recent years, St. George has been the parish of choice for middle-class families building new homes.

St. Lucy and St. Peter

Both of these parishes are located on the north coast of Barbados, an area that boasts some dramatic scenery, from the rough waters of the Atlantic to sleepy Bajan villages and herds of blackbelly sheep. St. Peter Parish is home to Speightstown, the second-largest town in Barbados. The island's first major port, Speightstown is the only settlement that retains its original layout of streets.

In both of these parishes, pricey tourist resorts have sprung up near remnants of Barbados's colonial past. Among the highlights is the 350-year-old St. Nicholas Abbey, one of the oldest structures on the island. It was also in this part of the island that artifacts from Barbados's earliest people were found. The buried pieces of pottery set the known date of the island's original settlement back more than 2,000 years.

A Calendar of Barbadian Festivals

January

January 1, **New Year's Day**, is an official holiday in Barbados.

Later in the month, on January 21, Bajans celebrate **Errol Barrow Day**. Barrow, a longtime prime minister, is considered the father of Barbados's independence.

January is also important to lovers of water sports, as it is the month when the **Barbados Windsurfing World Cup** takes place.

February

In mid-February, Bajans celebrate the **Holetown Festival**, which commemorates the founding of the first English settlement on Barbados in February 1627. Highlights of the weeklong festival include beauty contests, parades, art exhibitions, concerts, and theatrical presentations.

March

Christian Bajans, who make up about 7 in 10 of the island's residents, attend religious services on **Good Friday** and **Easter**. (These religious holidays may also fall in April.)

Easter weekend is also the time for the **Oistins Fish Festival**, held in the southeastern town of Oistins to honor the contributions of the island's fishermen. In addition to sampling traditional Bajan fare such as fish cakes and fried fish, visitors and locals alike can watch the fish-boning competition, dance to the beat of reggae and calypso music, and peruse the work of local artists and craftspeople.

April

The 28th of the month is **Heroes Day**, a time for Bajans to celebrate the lives and accomplishments of 10 national heroes, including political leaders Grantley Adams and Errol Barrow, and cricket superstars Sir Garfield Sobers and Sir Frank Leslie Walcott.

In late April, Christ Church Parish hosts the **Congaline Carnival**, whose highlights include concerts by calypso and reggae musicians from throughout the Caribbean, arts and crafts, and local food.

May

On May 1, Bajans celebrate **Labour Day**, honoring the contributions of all workers.

July

Most of the events of the **Crop Over Festival**, a weeks-long national celebration of Bajan culture, take place in July. The festival features food, parades, music competitions, and art and photography exhibits.

August

Emancipation Day, commemorating the freeing of Barbados's black slaves in 1834, is celebrated on August 1.

The first Monday of the month is **Kadooment Day**, the climax of the Crop Over

A Calendar of Barbadian Festivals

Festival. Elaborately costumed calypso bands march in a parade and compete for prizes.

October

On the first Monday of the month, Bajans mark **United Nations Day**. Barbados joined the international organization in 1966, shortly after gaining its independence.

November

November in Barbados offers something for aficionados of the performing arts and sports fans alike. The **National Independence Festival of Creative Arts** includes music, singing, drama, and dance competitions. The **Caribbean Surfing Championship** draws participants and spectators from throughout the region.

On November 30, Bajans celebrate **Independence Day**. Barbados gained its independence from Great Britain in 1966.

December

December 25 is the Christian holiday of **Christmas**, commemorating the birth of Jesus. In Barbados it is a day for giving gifts to loved ones.

Boxing Day, December 26, is a public holiday in Barbados, as in other parts of the British Commonwealth. Tradition holds that on this day, English nobles would box up presents for their servants, and churches would open alms boxes for the poor.

The Bright Ledge reef is a popular spot for divers.

Recipes

Lime Sweet Bread
1 1/2 cup flour
1/2 tsp salt
1 tsp baking powder
1 1/4 cup granulated sugar
1/2 cup melted butter
2 eggs
Juice and grated rind of 1 large lime
Glaze:
1/2 cup icing sugar
Juice and grated rind of 1 lime

Directions:
1. Combine all ingredients, mixing until sugar is dissolved. Set aside.
2. Preheat oven to 350°F.
3. Grease a 9"x 5" x 3" loaf pan; set aside.
4. Place all ingredients in a food processor. Process until well combined.
5. Pour into pan and bake for 1 hour. Remove from pan and while still warm, prick all over with toothpick and pour the glaze over it.
Best served chilled.

(Recipe from Laurelann Morely, chef at "The Cove" in St. Joseph, Barbados)

Coconut Sugar Cakes
1/2 lb grated coconut
1/4 pint water
3/4 lb sugar

Directions:
1. Place the sugar in a saucepan and add water. Simmer until the sugar melts and then add the coconut. Let boil slowly, stirring constantly to avoid burning. Allow to cook until it thickens and takes on a greasy look.
2. Drop the mixture by tablespoons onto a shallow plate or cookie sheet that has been moistened with water.
3. Let it set before eating.

Corn Pie
1 tbsp sugar
1 1/2 tbsp sifted flour
1/2 lb Anchor cheese, grated
1 can of corn, drained
1/2 can of evaporated milk
1 egg
1 onion, finely chopped
1/2 sweet pepper, finely chopped
1 tbsp butter

Directions:
1. Melt the butter in the pan and add the flour. Stir to avoid lumps.
2. Add milk, stirring constantly to avoid lumps, and then add grated cheese. Next, add corn, sugar, and onion. Add egg last.
3. Bake in oven at 350°F for 35–40 minutes.

Bajan Rice and Stew

8 oz. stew beef
1 large carrot, peeled and sliced
2 medium potatoes, peeled and quartered
2 tbsp Bajan seasoning
1/4 tsp seasoned salt
1 tbsp gravy browning
2 tbsp ketchup
1 cup water
2 tbsp vegetable oil
2 cups long-grain rice, soaked in water for two hours
1/2 cup pigeon peas, soaked in water overnight
1 oz. salt pork
1/2 tsp thyme
4 cups water

Directions:

For the stew:
1. Wash and cut beef into bite-sized pieces and then rub with seasoning and ketchup.
2. Heat oil in a skillet and stir-fry meat for 10 minutes. Pour in the gravy browning and cook for another 5 minutes. Add water, cover, and simmer for 30 minutes.
3. Stir in the carrot and potatoes, adjust the seasonings with salt, and cook another 15 minutes. Add more water if necessary. The meat should be done after about 45 minutes of cooking.

For the rice:
1. Place the peas, salt pork, and thyme in a pan with 4 cups of water and bring to a boil. Reduce heat and simmer for 30 minutes or until the peas are tender.
2. Wash and drain the rice and add to the pan. Pour in enough water to just cover the mixture. Bring to a boil and then reduce the heat to low.
3. Cover and simmer for about 20 minutes or until the water is gone.

Peanut Punch

1/3 cup smooth peanut butter
14-oz. can evaporated milk
14-oz. can condensed milk
1 cup water
1 tbsp sugar
1 egg
1 tsp vanilla
1 cup milk
Peel of lime or lemon

Directions:

1. Mix the peanut butter with the evaporated milk. Add condensed milk and water and mix well. Taste it and if not sweet enough, add some sugar.
2. Beat egg with peel and then throw away the peel.
3. Add egg mixture and milk to peanut butter mixture.
4. Bottle, chill, and serve with ice.

Glossary

aviary—a place where birds are kept.

brig—a military prison.

by-products—secondary products of a manufacturing or chemical process.

calypso—a type of music that originated in the West Indies and that often pokes fun at local political figures.

cholera—a severe, sometimes fatal intestinal infection that is caused by a type of bacteria.

conch shell—a large, spiral-shaped shell.

dreadlocks—a hairstyle consisting of long, rope-like strands formed by braiding the hair.

duppies—ghosts or spirits.

emancipation—the act of freeing, especially from slavery.

mulatto—a person of mixed white and black ancestry.

obeah—witchcraft; black magic.

parasailing—a recreational activity during which a person harnessed to a parachute and tethered to a powerboat is lifted into the air.

parish—a political and administrative division of territory similar to a state or county.

radiocarbon dating—a method of determining the approximate age of very old objects by measuring the amount of a form of carbon they contain.

Rastafarian—a member of an Afro-Caribbean religious group that venerates the former emperor of Ethiopia, Haile Selassie; forbids the cutting of hair; and stresses black culture and identity.

reggae—a popular music of Jamaican origin having elements of calypso and rhythm and blues.

stalactites—icicle-like formations hanging from a cave's roof.

stalagmites—cone-shaped deposits on a cave's floor.

synagogue—a Jewish house of worship.

Project and Report Ideas

Nature Reports

- Go to the library or search the Internet for information about the unusual kinds of trees found in Barbados. Sketch the various species and write a report on how they differ, what kind of fruit they produce (if any), and other interesting facts.
- The green monkeys of Barbados are a major nuisance to farmers. Find out more information about these primates. When were they introduced into Barbados? Why have they flourished on the island? What damage do they do, and how have farmers and the government responded to the problem in the past? Write up a management plan that suggests ways of controlling the green monkeys.

Just Imagine

Write a story (fiction) about what may have happened to the Arawak and Carib inhabitants of Barbados. Experts have theories to explain the mysterious disappearances of these two peoples, but no definitive proof exists. Make your story clever and creative!

You're Invited!

Imagine that you have been invited to go to Barbados for a vacation. What would you like to see and do there? Search the Internet or some travel books to find information about the different places of interest. Then, using a map of the country, plan a seven-day dream vacation on the island.

Hurricane Season Again

From time to time, major hurricanes strike Barbados. Make a list of the steps you think Bajans would need to take to minimize the damage to their property and the risk to their safety. Explain your logic clearly.

Design a Word

Bajans are known for creating unusual words. A "sea-bath," for example, means a swim in the ocean. Make up some new Bajan words for things that might be found on the island (sugarcane, green monkeys, sugar apples, and mangrove trees, for example). Create a list of at least 15 words.

Cooking Time

Pick one of the recipes in this book and try making it (with parental help and permission, of course!). Write a report on: how difficult it was to make, how easy it was to find the ingredients, how it tasted, and what you did and did not like.

Flying the Flag

Find a picture of the Barbados flag and draw it in full color. Label each part and explain what it stands for. If possible, include the history of how it was selected.

Story Time

Imagine that you are one of the thousands of African slaves who were brought to Barbados to work on the sugar plantations. Write a diary (about two weeks' worth of entries) revealing what your life is like.

Chronology

Ca. 3000 B.C. Amerindians arrive on Barbados and begin to settle the island; their culture is known to have included fishing and tools made from conch shells.

400–200 B.C. An Amerindian people originally from South America, the Arawaks, migrate to Barbados.

Ca. A.D. 1200 Arawaks disappear from Barbados; another group, the Caribs, begin 300-year occupation of the island.

1511 An official document issued by King Ferdinand of Spain authorizing the capture of slaves lists Barbados for the first time.

1536 Portuguese navigator Pedro a Campos sails to uninhabited Barbados and names it "the bearded one" for the shaggy fig trees along the shoreline.

1625 Captain John Powell lands at present-day Holetown and claims the island for James I, king of England; two years later his brother, Captain William Powell, establishes the first English settlement.

1628 Bridgetown is founded.

1637 Sugarcane is first brought to the island, from Brazil.

1639 Barbados's first colonial legislature is established.

1647 Yellow fever epidemic kills 6,000 people.

1663 First organized uprising of blacks occurs; over the next 40 years, periodic uprisings will take place.

1766 Bridgetown is destroyed by fire.

1834 Emancipation Act abolishes slavery on the island.

1854 Cholera epidemic hits, killing 20,000.

1898 A hurricane destroys 18,000 homes.

1902	Smallpox outbreak.
1908	Yellow fever epidemic hits.
1938	Grantley H. Adams founds the Barbados Labour Party.
1961	Great Britain grants Barbados complete control of its internal affairs; Errol Barrow is elected the island's first president.
1966	Barbados gains independence, becoming a member nation of the British Commonwealth; joins the United Nations.
1967	Barbados joins the Organization of American States.
1986	Errol Barrow becomes prime minister for the second time.
1987	Barrow dies in office; L. Erskine Sandiford becomes prime minister.
1992	Economic crisis brings island to the edge of bankruptcy.
1994	Owen Arthur becomes prime minister; five years later he is reelected.
2000	Unemployment rate drops below 10 percent for the first time in more than 25 years.
2001	In December, Prime Minister Owen Arthur speaks at the third summit of heads of state of the Association of Caribbean States.
2002	Barbados hosts the Caribbean Geological Conference in June.

Further Reading/Internet Resources

Broberg, Merle. *Barbados*. Philadelphia: Chelsea House, 1998.

Elias, Marie Louise. *Barbados*. Salt Lake City, Utah: Benchmark Books, 2000.

Gantos, Jack. *Jack's New Power: Stories from a Caribbean Year*. New York: Farrar, Straus and Giroux, 1995.

Gunning, Monica. *Not a Copper Penny in Me House*: *Poems of the Caribbean.* Honesdale, Pa.: Boyds Mills Press, 1993.

Travel Information

http://www.barbados.org
http://www.funbarbados.com
http://barbados2000.com
http://www.insandoutsofbarbados.com

History and Geography

http://www.cia.gov/cia/publications/factbook/geos/bb.html
http://www.bartelby.com/151/c23.html

Political and Economic Information

http://www.barbados.gov.bb/
http://www.globalbarbados.com
http://travel.state.gov/barbados.html

Culture and Festivals

http://landmarks-and-festivals-of-barbados.visit-barbados.com/
http://www.lonelyplanet.com/destinations/caribbean/barbados/facts.htm#event

For More Information

Embassy of Barbados
2144 Wyoming Ave., NW
Washington, DC 20008
202-939-9200
202-332-7467 (Fax)
Website: http://www.embassy.org/embassies/bb.html

Barbados Tourism Authority
U.S. Office
3440 Wiltshire Blvd., Suite 1215
Los Angeles, CA 90010
213-380-2198 or 213-380-2199
213-384-2763 (Fax)
Website: http://www.barbados.org/usa

Barbados Immigration Department
Careenage House, The Wharf
Bridgetown, Barbados
246-426-1011
Website: http://www.barbados.org/relocate.htm

Index

Page
2:      © OTTN Publishing
3:      © OTTN Publishing
7:      Photo Disc
8:      Dave G. Houser/Houserstock
9:      Dave G. Houser/Houserstock
10:     Jan Butchofsky-Houser/Houserstock
13:     Dave G. Houser/Houserstock
14:     Jonathan Blair/Corbis
16:     Corbis
17:     Jonathan Blair/Corbis
18:     Gianni Dagli Orti/Corbis
23:     Hulton/Archive/Getty Images
24:     Rafael Perez/Reuters/Getty Images
26:     Wolfgang Kaehler/Corbis

27:     Dave G. Houser/Houserstock
29:     Jonathan Blair/Corbis
30:     Jonathan Blair/Corbis
34:     Dave G. Houser/Houserstock
35:     Dave G. Houser/Corbis
37:     Tony Arruza/Corbis
40:     Hulton/Archive/Getty Images
41:     Franz-Marc Frei/Corbis
42:     Jonathan Blair/Corbis
43:     Dave G. Houser/Houserstock
45:     Jonathan Blair/Corbis
46:     Tony Arruza/Corbis
51:     Corbis Images

Cover photos: (front) Dave G. Houser/Houserstock; (back) Corbis Images

Contributors

Senior Consulting Editor **James D. Henderson** is professor of international studies at Coastal Carolina University. He is the author of *Conservative Thought in Twentieth Century Latin America: The Ideals of Laureano Gómez* (1988; Spanish edition *Las ideas de Laureano Gómez* published in 1985); *When Colombia Bled: A History of the Violence in Tolima* (1985; Spanish edition *Cuando Colombia se desangró, una historia de la Violencia en metrópoli y provincia*, 1984); and coauthor of *A Reference Guide to Latin American History* (2000) and *Ten Notable Women of Latin America* (1978).

Mr. Henderson earned a bachelor's degree in history from Centenary College of Louisiana, and a master's degree in history from the University of Arizona. He then spent three years in the Peace Corps, serving in Colombia, before earning his doctorate in Latin American history in 1972 at Texas Christian University.

Tamra Orr lives in Portland, Oregon. She is the author of more than a half dozen non-fiction books for children and families, including *A Parent's Guide to Homeschooling* (Mars Publishing, 2002). In her spare time, she enjoys reading and talking to her children and husband, who teach her something new every day.